The Life and Trial of Lizzie Borden: America's Most Famous Murder Case

By Charles River Editors

Lizzie Borden

About Charles River Editors

Charles River Editors provides superior editing and original writing services across the digital publishing industry, with the expertise to create digital content for publishers across a vast range of subject matter. In addition to providing original digital content for third party publishers, we also republish civilization's greatest literary works, bringing them to new generations of readers via ebooks.

Sign up here to receive updates about free books as we publish them, and visit Our Kindle Author Page to browse today's free promotions and our most recently published Kindle titles.

Introduction

Lizzie Borden (1860-1927)

"Lizzie Borden took an axe

Gave her mother forty whacks,

Then she hid behind the door,

And gave her father forty more." – Contemporary nursery rhyme

"Lizzie Borden took an axe, and gave her mother forty whacks, when she saw what she had done, she gave her father forty-one." Like so many others, this ditty and similar ones sacrificed accuracy in the name of rhyme and rhythm, as Abby and Andrew Borden were not hit 81 times but "only" 29. Of course, that still proved to be more than enough to kill both of them and propel their daughter, Elizabeth, into infamy.

Today, cases are often referred to as the trial of the century, but few could lay claim in the 19th century like Lizzie Borden's in the wake of her parents' murders. After all, the story included the grisly axe murders of wealthy socialites and a young daughter as the prime suspect. As Trey

Wyatt, author of *The Life, Legend, and Mystery of Lizzie Borden*, put it, "Women were held to strict standards and genteel women were pampered, while at the same time they were expected to behave within a strict code of conduct. In 1892, Fall River, Massachusetts wealthy society ladies were not guilty of murder, and if they did kill someone, it would not be with an axe."

When questioned, Lizzie gave contradictory accounts to the police, which ultimately helped lead to her arrest and trial, but supporters claimed it may have been the effects of morphine that she had a prescription to take. Much like subsequent famous murder cases, such as the O.J. Simpson case or Leopold & Loeb, Lizzie Borden's trial garnered national attention unlike just about anything that had come before. The case sparked Americans' interest in legal proceedings, and as with Simpson, even an acquittal didn't take the spotlight off the Borden case, which has been depicted in all forms of media ever since. Lizzie became a pariah among contemporaries who believed she'd escaped justice, and she remains the prime suspect, but the unsolved nature of the case has allowed other writers to advance other theories and point at other suspects.

The Life and Trial of Lizzie Borden: The History of 19th Century America's Most Famous Murder Case looks at the personal background of the Borden family and the shocking true crime that captivated America at the end of the 19th century. Along with pictures of important people, places, and events, you will learn about Dali like never before, in no time at all.

The Life and Trial of Lizzie Borden: The History of 19th Century America's Most Famous Murder Case

About Charles River Editors

Introduction

   Chapter 1: The Borden Family

   Chapter 2: Prelude to Tragedy

   Chapter 3: 29 Whacks

   Chapter 4: The Investigation

   Chapter 5: Inquest, Arrest, Indictment

   Chapter 6: The Trial

   Online Resources

   Bibliography

Chapter 1: The Borden Family

"In 1892, Fall River, Massachusetts was a sprawling industrial town only 49 miles South of Boston. Textile mills powered by the Taunton River and worked by thousands of immigrants, made the town prosperous. Fall River was the second largest (Manchester, England was the largest) textile manufacturing center in the world. The thriving mills and the busy port resulted in an economic boom, throughout the 1870's, which created a handful of wealthy families that lived in the elegant 'Highlands' neighborhood known as 'The Hill'. The Women's Suffrage Movement was growing by leaps and bounds in New York City, but it would be 1920 before women had the right to vote…Fall River was a center of industry that grew into a cultural oasis funded by the 'new money' of the founding families. Families like the Durfees, the Braytons, the Davols, the Chases, the Remingtons and the Bordens were at the heart of every business, church service, cultural event and election." - Trey Wyatt, *The Life, Legend, and Mystery of Lizzie Borden*

Part of what made the Borden murders so shocking was the social context in which they took place, because prior to that dreadful day, the Borden's were the typical upper-middle class American family. Andrew and his first wife, Sarah Morse, were married on Christmas Day in 1845 when he was 23 years old, and they lived at 92 Second Street in Fall River, Massachusetts, a decent part of town where they could still live in the very frugal manner that Andrew preferred. Their first child, Emma, was born in 1851, and she was followed nine years later by Lizzie Andrew on July 19, 1860. A third child, Alice, was born sometime between the two surviving sisters but died very young. According to one article published in *The Boston Herald* at the time of the murders, "Lizzie was born in the old family homestead on Ferry St., in which her father has lived and his father before him. It is the same estate which the dead Andrew J. Borden deeded to the two girls in 1887. As a child she was of a very sensitive nature, inclined to be non-communicative with new acquaintances, and this characteristic has tenaciously clung to her all through life, and has been erroneously interpreted. Her sister, being older, was a constant guide and an idolized companion. An unusual circumstance is that of her practically having no choice of friends until she attained womanhood."

A 19th century picture of the Borden house at 92 Second St. in Fall River

A modern picture of the house

Pictures of Andrew Borden

SARAH ANTHONY MORSE BORDEN WITH BABY EMMA LENORA

Sarah and baby Emma

Emma Borden

Young Lizzie Borden

The fact that the couple went so many years without children suggests a number of miscarriages or some sort of marital estrangement, either of which would have put excessive pressure on the young couple, and the fact that Lizzie was given her father's name indicates that the two, who had been married by this time for 15 years, held out little hope for a male heir. Two years later, in March 1863, Sarah passed away of "uterine congestion- 4 mos.- and disease of the spine," likely some form of cancer perhaps exacerbated by yet another miscarriage.

The only other significant family member in Lizzie's life was her uncle, John Morse, who remained close to Andrew following his sister's death and may have been the man's only real friend. They were even in business together, and Morse lived with the family for most of 1875. He later told one reporter, "My sister Sarah A. Morse, married Andrew Borden in the city of Fall River when both were, as I remember, in their 22d year. ... At that time Mr. Borden was in reduced circumstances and was just beginning to enter business. They lived for years on Ferry Street. ... Mr. Borden first went into the furniture business on Anawan Street, where he remained for 30 years or more. My sister died 28 years ago. At that time Mr. Borden was worth fully $150,000, which amount he had invested largely in mill stocks, which were highly paying securities. He told me on one occasion that he had $78,000 in mill stocks alone. He afterwards invested heavily in a horsecar line…"

Morse

Andrew, consumed with a manufacturing business making huge profits off of the American Civil War, often left his younger daughter in the care of her sister or a hired woman. It was not until the war was over that he decided to remarry, bringing his new wife Abby into the family in June 1865. The 37 year old woman had never married and might have looked to Andrew to improve her own social status, and for his part, Andrew needed a wife to run his home and a mother for his children.

Abby Borden

Lizzie soon began calling Abby mother, having little to no memory of Sarah, but 14 year old Emma did not fare so well and was eventually packed off to boarding school. This was particularly hard on Lizzie, who later said of Abby, "I had never been to her as a mother in many things. I always went to my sister because she was older and had the care of me after my mother died."

In speaking of Lizzie, Horace Benson, her school principal, said to a reporter, "as a pupil she was an average scholar, neither being exceptionally smart nor noticeably dull. She was subject to varying moods, and was never fond of her stepmother. She had no hesitation in talking about her, and in many ways showed her dislike of her father's second wife." Benson also described Abby as "a kindly, lovable woman, who tried, but ineffectually, to win the love of the stepdaughters." *The Boston Herald* article mentioned above also observed, "At the usual age she was sent to the Morgan Street School, embracing primary and grammar grades. Her school days were perhaps unlike most girls in this lack of affiliation with her fellow pupils. As a scholar she was not remarkable for brilliancy, but she was conscientious in her studies and with application always held a good rank in her class. She entered the high school when about 15 or 16 years old. … Her life was uneventful during the few years following her leaving school. She abandoned her piano music lessons because, although making encouraging progress, she conceived the idea that she was not destined to become a good musician. … Her father and mother were religious and regular church attendants, and she has been surrounded by Christian Home influences. When a young girl, she accompanied her parents to Chicago and was there a member of the Sunday school class and punctual in attendance. She was, however, a girl with anything but an enthusiastic idea of her own personal attainments. She thought people were not favorably disposed toward her and that she made a poor impression. This conduced to the acceptance of this very opinion among church people, and consequently the young woman was to some extent avoided by the young women of the church."

As Lizzie reached her teen years, she did what most girls that age do by gravitating toward her father, shutting out her stepmother, and clinging to her older sister Emma, who remained in the home and never married. Lizzie also enjoyed an active social life appropriate for a young woman of her time and status (by this time, her father had made a lot of money during the war and was considered one of the town's leading citizens). Lizzie attended parties and took a leadership role in many of the clubs around town, serving as Secretary of the Fruit and Flower Mission. She was also active in the life of the Central Congregational Church, which she joined in 1885.

Like Emma, Lizzie was destined to be a spinster, and over time something of a power struggle erupted between the three women living together in the same house. When Lizzie was 27, she and Abby had a falling out, after which Lizzie stopped referring to her as mother. *The Boston Herald* article noted, "There was a remarkable change in her some five years ago and at that time she first began to fraternize with church people. Then, of course, when she was thoroughly understood, when the obnoxiously retiring manner was dissipated and the responsive nature of the girl came to view, she became at once popular and then came the acquisition of the friends who today sound her praises." On June 21, 1890, Lizzie and Emma left Boston for a 19 week European tour, and while this is not particularly surprising considering their age and income, it might also be indicative of a desire to get away from unhappiness at home.

Though there were three adult women living in the home, the Borden's still employed domestic help to handle the more grueling housekeeping tasks. In 1889, they hired a young Irish immigrant named Bridget Sullivan as a type of maid-of-all-work. She later testified, "In the household I was sometimes called Maggie, by Miss Emma and Miss Lizzie. … Was born in Ireland; came first to Newport, Rhode Island. After a year there, went to South Bethlehem, Pennsylvania. I came to Fall River four years ago; went to work for Mrs. Reed. Had been working for Mr. Borden two years and nine months at the time of his death. There was no other domestic servant, but a man from the farm used to come and do chores; his first name was Alfred; I don't know his other name. They used to keep a horse in the barn until about a year before Mr. Borden died. After the horse went they didn't use the barn for anything. My work was washing, ironing and cooking and sweeping. I did not have the care of any of the bedchambers except my own. My room was in the third story, right over Mr. Borden's, and his was over the kitchen."

Sullivan

Chapter 2: Prelude to Tragedy

"By 1892, both sisters had never been married. Lizzie was 32 and Emma was 42. Their hopes were slipping away. Although they had a live-in housemaid, the women were responsible for portions of the housework and they all cleaned their own rooms. Lizzie was not living the life she had always envisioned for herself. Lizzie and Emma felt entitled to the lifestyle and surroundings that their 'founding family' status could have provided them. It is possible that the recent 'Grand Tour' of Europe that Lizzie took, with some of her Fall River friends, opened up new hopes and dreams. She traveled for three months to all of the capitals of Europe, saw all the amazing art museums, experienced the glamour and glitter of European high society and met expatriots living abroad. The return home to Second Street could have been devastating. Lizzie was always more outgoing than Emma. She was also more likely to voice her opinions to their father and step-mother. There had long been rumors that Lizzie was suspected of shoplifting items from the local stores. Whether this was a symptom of deeper problems or a reflection of the 'entitlement' issue is not really known. When her thefts surfaced from the local shopkeepers, it is believed that Andrew paid for whatever was taken." - Trey Wyatt, *The Life, Legend, and Mystery of Lizzie Borden*

During the months and days leading up to the gruesome murders, a number of events took place that, when seen in the light of what followed, seem to be harbingers of doom. The first occurred on June 24, 1891, the day Andrew and Abby travelled out of town to their farm in Swansea, Massachusetts while Lizzie and Emma remained at home with Sullivan. It was a big day for Lizzie, who was being named to the Board of the local Good Samaritan Hospital, but at some point the house was robbed, apparently while the three women were there. Alice Russell, the next door neighbor, later testified that Lizzie talked to her about that day: "I have forgotten where she had been. She said, 'And you know the barn has been broken into twice.' And I said, 'Oh well, you know well that that was somebody after pigeons; there is nothing in there for them to go after but pigeons.' 'Well,' she says, 'they have broken into the house in broad daylight, with Emma and Maggie and me there.' And I said, 'I never heard of that before.' And she said, 'Father forbade our telling it.' So I asked her about it, and she said it was in Mrs. Borden's room, what she called her dressing room. She said her things were ransacked, and they took a watch and chain and money and car tickets, and something else that I can't remember. And there was a nail left in the keyhole; she didn't know why that was left; whether they got in with it or what. I asked her if her father did anything about it, and she said he gave it to the police, but they didn't find out anything; and she said father expected that they would catch the thief by the tickets. She remarked, 'Just as if anybody would use those tickets.'"

By this time, Lizzie was considered something of a troubled soul by her family and had been previously accused of shoplifting. Therefore, the family suspected that she might actually have been the thief herself. No one else was ever accused, and Mr. Borden soon had locks installed on the doors to every room in the house but allowed Sullivan a key to the side door.

Needless to say, relations within the family remained tense, but everyone continued to perform their expected roles, at least when outside the home. Lizzie remained active in community affairs and was even made the Treasurer of Young Woman's Christian Temperance Union in Fall River. Her façade cracked only briefly when she confided to a friend that she considered her stepmother "a mean old thing."

A few months later, there was more suspicious activity around the home when, in April 1892, the Borden barn was broken into. Claiming that they had attracted the intruders, Andrew Borden decided to do away with the pigeons that lived in his barn; in spite of the fact that Lizzie considered them pets, he used a hatchet to kill most of them. This only intensified the resentment that had grown between them.

According to Lizzie, she was not the only one who had problems with her father at this time. She later testified at the inquest that just weeks before the murders, a mysterious man visited the home. "I heard the bell ring and father went to the door and let him in. I did not hear anything for some time except just the voices. Then I heard the man say, 'I would like to have that place; I would like to have that store.' Father said, 'I am not willing to let your business go in there.' And the man said, 'I thought with your reputation for liking money, you would let your store for anything.' Father said, 'You are mistaken.' Then they talked a while and then their voices were louder and I heard father order him out and went to the front door with him. … I think it was a man from out of town because he said he was going home to see his partner."

A few weeks later, both Emma and Lizzie left home for an extended trip, perhaps hoping to get some perspective or even make plans for the future, but even though they traveled to New Bedford together, the two sisters stayed with different friends. During this time, Lizzie made a number of day trips by herself. For instance, she went shopping alone on July 23 and then to visit a friend, the wealthy Charles W. Anthony, on his yacht on July 25. The following day, she returned to Fall River, while Emma remained with friends in Fairhaven.

By this time, Andrew and Abby Borden had less than a week to live, and a number of other suspicious events began to occur. First, after working in the home for more than three years, Sullivan suddenly decided to serve mutton for Sunday dinner. This anomaly would have escaped notice if not for the fact that the meat was known for its strong flavor, which could easily mask an unsavory ingredient. This seems to have been on Abby's mind when, a few days later, she and Andrew fell ill. After a substantial breakfast on the morning of August 3, she visited Dr. Seabury Bowen, who lived just across the street, and complained to him that she was feeling ill and that she suspected that she and her husband were being poisoned. Dr. Bowen went back to the house to visit Andrew but was unable to see him. According to her friend Alice Russell, Lizzie told her, "Dr. Bowen came over. Mrs. Borden went over, and Father didn't like it because she was going; and she told him where she was going, and he says, 'Well, my money shan't pay for it.' She went over to Dr. Bowen's, and Dr. Bowen told her—she told him she was afraid they were poisoned—and Dr. Bowen laughed, and said, No, there wasn't any poison. And she came back, and Dr. Bowen came over.' And she said, 'I am so ashamed, the way Father treated Dr.

Bowen. I was so mortified.' And she said after he had gone Mrs. Borden said she thought it was too bad for him to treat Dr. Bowen so, and he said he didn't want him coming over there that way."

During this time, Lizzie also told Sullivan she herself had been ill, but according to at least one witness, Eli Bence, Lizzie went out shopping that morning. In fact, Bence claimed Lizzie stopped by D. R. Smith's drugstore to purchase a bottle of prussic acid, also known as cyanide, but that he would not sell it to her.

That day at noon, Sullivan served up more mutton for lunch, dishing up the leftover mutton soup for dinner. Morse also showed up that day, and he later explained, "Wednesday I came here from New Bedford early in the afternoon. ... Andrew was then reclining on the sofa in about the position he was found murdered. He looked up and laughed saying, 'Hello, John, is that you? Have you been to dinner' I replied in the negative. Mrs. Borden interrupted Mr. Borden, saying: 'Sit right down, we are just through and everything is hot on the stove. It won't cost us a mite of trouble.' They sat by my side through dinner, and then I told them I was going over to Kirby's stable and get a team to drive over to Luther's. I invited Andrew to go, but he denied, saying he didn't feel well enough. He asked me to bring him over some eggs from his farm which is there located...."

After he left, Lizzie remained at home for a while before going over to pay a call on her friend, Alice Russell, who later testified, "[Lizzie] said, 'I have taken your advice, and I have written to Marion that I will come.' I don't know what came in between, I don't know as this followed that, but I said, 'I am glad you are going,' as I had urged her to go before. And I don't know just what followed, but I said something about her having a good time, and she said, 'Well, I don't know; I feel depressed. I feel as if something was hanging over me that I cannot throw off, and it comes over me at times, no matter where I am.' And she says, 'When I was at the table the other day, when I was at Marion, the girls were laughing and talking and having a good time, and this feeling came over me, and one of them spoke and said, 'Lizzie, why don't you talk?'"

This seems a strange concern for a woman well into her 30s and more like something a schoolgirl would worry about. However, there were stranger comments to come. Russell continued, "[Lizzie] said, 'Mr. and Mrs. Borden were awfully sick last night.' And I said, 'Why, what is the matter; something they have eaten?' She said, 'We were all sick,' she said, 'all but Maggie.' And I said, 'Something you think you have eaten?' She said, 'We don't know. We had some baker's bread, and all ate of it but Maggie, and Maggie wasn't sick.' And I said, 'Well, it couldn't have been the bread; if it had been baker's bread I should suppose other people would be sick, and I haven't heard of anybody.' And she says, 'That is so.' And she says, 'Sometimes I think our milk might be poisoned.' ... And then I said-I asked her what time the milk came, if she knew. She said, 'I think about four o'clock.' And I said, 'Well, it is light at four. I shouldn't think anybody would dare to come then and tamper with the cans for fear somebody would see them.' And she said, 'I shouldn't think so.' And she said, 'They were awfully sick; and I wasn't sick, I didn't vomit; but I heard them vomiting and stepped to the door and asked if I could do anything, and they said, No. ... Well, I think she told me that they were better in the morning and that Mrs. Borden thought that they had been poisoned, and she went over to Dr. Bowen's—said she was going over to Dr. Bowen's."

When the poison story began to fall flat, Lizzie moved on to another disturbing topic. According to Alice Russell, "[Lizzie] says, 'I feel afraid sometimes that Father has got an enemy. Father,' she said, 'he has so much trouble with his men that come to see him.' She told me of a man that came to see him, and she heard him say-she didn't see him, but heard her father say, 'I don't care to let my property for such business.' And she said the man answered sneeringly, 'I shouldn't think you would care what you let your property for.' And she said, 'Father was mad and ordered him out of the house.' She told me of seeing a man run around the house one night when she went home. ... She said, 'I feel as if I wanted to sleep with my eyes half open—with one eye open half the time—-for fear they will burn the house down over us. ... I think sometimes—I am afraid sometimes that somebody will do something to him; he is so discourteous to people.'"

By the time Lizzie returned to the house that evening, Morse was also there, and he stayed over for the night. Abby retired at 9:15, just a little while after Lizzie returned, and the rest of the household went to bed a little after 10:00.

Chapter 3: 29 Whacks

"On the day of the murder, Bridget Sullivan was sick. She had not suffered any symptoms before then, but she was throwing up and feeling dizzy on August 4, after she ate breakfast. The cause of the family illness was a mystery. There was testimony that Lizzie tried to buy prussic acid the day before the murder. The witness also said that he had turned her away and would not sell it to her. There were many speculations that Lizzie had been poisoning her family and when it didn't work that she resorted to the hatchet. There are a couple of things wrong with this theory. First, there was no proof that she ever bought any poison, and none was found anywhere on the Borden's property. Secondly, when the autopsies were done on the contents of Abby and Andrew's stomachs, no poison was found." - Trey Wyatt, *The Life, Legend, and Mystery of Lizzie Borden.*

August 4, 1892 would become one of the most famous days in the history of true crime, and historian Trey Wyatt set the scene in his book on Lizzie Borden: "So the family had deep undercurrents of conflict. Every relationship in the house was strained, with the exception of Lizzie and Emma's. The women hated their step-mother and her extended family, and they wanted to move up to a mansion on 'The Hill'".

That said, the morning of August 4, 1892 began like any other morning in the household, with the older adults getting up first and having breakfast together at around 7:00. Sullivan later testified, "Mrs. Borden was the first one I see that morning; she gave me orders about breakfast; it was about half-past six. Mr. Borden came down in about five minutes; he went into the sitting room and put the key of his bedroom on the shelf. ... He then came out into the kitchen, put on a dressing coat and went outdoors with a slop pail he had brought downstairs. ... I was in the kitchen; the windows of the kitchen look out into the back yard. Mr. Borden emptied the slop pail; then he unlocked the barn door and went into the barn. Then he went to the pear tree, picked up a basket of pears and brought them into the house. He washed up in the kitchen and went in to breakfast. When I put the breakfast on the table I saw Mr. Morse. For breakfast there was some mutton, some broth and johnnycakes, coffee and cookies. The broth was mutton broth."

For his part, Morse recalled, "It was about 6 o'clock when I got up, and had breakfast about an hour later. Then Andrew and I read the papers, and we chatted until about 9 o'clock. I am not positive as to the exact time, and it may have been only 8:45 o'clock. While at the table I asked Andrew why he did not buy Gould's yacht for $200,000, at which price it was advertised and he laughed, saying what little good it would do him if he really did have it. We also talked about business. I had come to Fall River, for one reason, to buy a pair of oxen for Butcher Davis, with whom I lived. He had wanted them, and I had agreed to take them on a certain day, but had not done so. Andrew told me when I was ready to go after them to write him at the farm, which would save him bothering in the matter."

While the men lingered at the table, Abby went off to get the day's work started. She was feeling fine, but Sullivan soon felt ill, as she later explained: "After they had their breakfast, I ate mine and commenced to clear things up. ... Five minutes later Miss Lizzie came through to the kitchen. I was washing the dishes and I asked her what did she want for breakfast. She said she didn't know as she wanted any breakfast, but she guessed she would have something, she guessed she would have some coffee and cookies. She got some coffee, and she was preparing to sit down at the kitchen table. I went out in the back yard. I had a sick headache and I was sick to my stomach. I went out to vomit, and I stayed ten or fifteen minutes."

By the time Lizzie was up at 9:00, Morse had left for the day, but she caught her father before he left and asked him to take a few letters to town with him to mail, and as he left the house, he assured her he would mail them. By 9:30, Abby had tidied the first floor rooms and had gone upstairs to continue her work, and she had already sent Sullivan out to wash the windows.

Sullivan was still doing that job when Andrew returned, and she remembered, "I heard like a person at the door was trying to unlock the door but could not; so I went to the front door and unlocked it. The spring lock was locked. I unbolted the door and it was locked with a key; there were three locks. I said 'pshaw,' and Miss Lizzie laughed, upstairs. Her father was out there on the doorstep. She was upstairs. She must have been either in the entry or at the top of the stairs, I can't tell which. Mr. Borden and I didn't say a word as he came in. I went back to my window washing; he came into the sitting room and went into the dining room. He had a little parcel in his hand, same as a paper or a book. He sat in a chair at the head of the lounge. Miss Lizzie came downstairs and came through the front entry into the dining room, I suppose to her father. I heard her ask her father if he had any mail, and they had some talk between them which I didn't understand, but I heard her tell her father that Mrs. Borden had a note and had gone out."

This seems untrue, because no one ever saw Abby Borden leave or return to the house that morning. Nonetheless, Sullivan continued, "The next thing I remember, Mr. Borden took a key off the mantelpiece and went up the back stairs. When he came downstairs again, I was finished in the sitting room, and I took my hand basin and stepladder into the dining room. I began to wash the dining-room windows. Then Miss Lizzie brought an ironing board from the kitchen, put it on the dining-room table and commenced to iron. She said, 'Maggie, are you going out this afternoon?' I said, 'I don't know; I might and I might not; I don't feel very well' She says, 'If you go out be sure and lock the door, for Mrs. Borden has gone out on a sick call, and I might go out, too.' Says I, 'Miss Lizzie, who is sick?' 'I don't know; she had a note this morning; it must be in town.' I finished my two windows; she went on ironing. Then I went in the kitchen, washed out my cloths and hung them behind the stove. Miss Lizzie came out there and said, 'There is a cheap sale of dress goods at Sergeant's this afternoon, at eight cents a yard.' … And I said, 'I am going to have one.' Then I went upstairs to my room. I don't remember to have heard a sound of anyone about the house, except those I named."

Lizzie, the last person to see her father alive and the first to see him dead, later claimed, "I asked him if he had any mail. He said, 'None for you.' He had a letter in his hand. I supposed it was for himself. I asked him how he felt. He said, 'About the same.' He said he should lie down. I asked him if he thought he should have a nap. He said he should try to. I asked him if he wanted the window left the way it was or if he felt a draught. He said, 'No.' ... He had laid down on the living room lounge, taken off his shoes and put on his slippers and taken off his coat and put on the reefer. I asked him if he wanted the window left that way. … Then I went into the kitchen and from there to the barn."

Believing that Abby was out of the house, and still not feeling well herself, Sullivan decided to take a short break from her work. It would be the last real rest she had for a long time. "Then I laid down in the bed. I heard the City Hall bell ring and I looked at my clock and it was eleven o'clock. I wasn't drowsing or sleeping. In my judgment I think I was there three or four minutes. I don't think I went to sleep at all. I heard no sound; I didn't hear the opening or closing of the screen door. I can hear that from my room if anyone is careless and slams the door. The next thing was that Miss Lizzie hollered, 'Maggie, come down!' I said, 'What is the matter?' She says, 'Come down quick; Father's dead; somebody came in and killed him.' This might be ten or fifteen minutes after the clock struck eleven, as far as I can judge."

A picture of Andrew Borden's body

Jumping up from her bed, Sullivan rushed downstairs, trying to process what she had just heard. She later testified, "When I got downstairs, I saw Miss Lizzie, standing with her back to the screen door. I went to go right in the sitting room and she says, 'Oh, Maggie, don't go in. I have got to have a doctor quick. Go over. I have got to have the doctor.' I went over to Dr. Bowen's right away, and when I came back, I says, 'Miss Lizzie, where was you?' I says, 'Didn't I leave the screen door hooked?' She says, 'I was out in the back yard and heard a groan, and came in and the screen door was wide open.' She says, 'Go and get Miss Russell. I can't be alone in the house.' So I got a hat and shawl and went. I had not found Dr. Bowen when I went to his house, but I told Mrs. Bowen that Mr. Borden was dead. I went to the house, corner of Borden and Second streets, learned that Miss Russell was not there; went to the cottage next the baker shop on Borden Street, and told Miss Russell. Then I came back to the Borden house."

Meanwhile, Adelaide Churchill, who lived next door, had seen Sullivan and felt that something was wrong. She later explained, "Miss Lizzie Borden was standing inside their screen door, at the side of their house. I opened the window and said, 'Lizzie, what is the matter?' She replied, 'Oh, Mrs. Churchill, do come over. Someone has killed Father.' I went over and stepped inside the screen door. She was sitting on the stair. I put my hand on her arm and said, 'Oh, Lizzie!' Then I said, 'Where is your father?' She said, 'In the sitting room.' And I said, 'Where were you when it happened?' and, she said, 'I went to the barn to get a piece of iron.' I said, 'Where is your mother?' She said, 'I don't know; she had got a note to go see someone who is sick, but I don't know but she is killed, too, for I thought I heard her come in.' She said, 'Father must have an enemy, for we have all been sick, and we think the milk has been poisoned... Dr. Bowen is not at home, and I must have a doctor.' I said, 'Lizzie, shall I go and try to get a doctor?' And she said, 'Yes,' and I went out."

By this time, Alice Russell had arrived. She later recalled, "Lizzie was there. I think she was standing in the door, leaning against the doorframe. I asked her to sit down in the rocking chair, which she did. ... People came around; I don't know who they were. ... I started to loosen her dress, thinking she was faint, and she said, 'I am not faint.' ... When Lizzie went upstairs, I went upstairs with her.... She had not yet changed her dress. She said, 'When it is necessary for an undertaker, I want Winwood.' I went downstairs and waited for Dr. Bowen. I sent for him, spoke to him, and went up to Lizzie's room again. She was coming out of Miss Emma's room, tying the ribbons of a wrapper-a pink-and-white striped wrapper."

When Dr. Bowen arrived, he found the household in chaos. He would testify, "I said, 'Lizzie, what is the matter?' She replied, 'Father has been killed', or 'stabbed'-I wouldn't say which it was. I said, 'Where is your father?' She answered, 'In the sitting room.' ... I saw the form of Mr. Borden lying on the lounge at the left of the sitting-room door. His face was very badly cut, apparently with a sharp instrument; his face was covered with blood. I felt of his pulse and satisfied myself he was dead. Glanced about the room and saw there was nothing disturbed; neither the furniture nor anything at all. Mr. Borden was lying with his face toward the south, on his right side, and apparently at ease, as if asleep. His face was hardly to be recognized by one who knew him. I made no other examination at the time, except to feel his pulse. Miss Lizzie had followed me part way through the dining room, and as I went back to the kitchen I asked her if she had seen anyone. She said, 'I have not.' Then I asked her, 'Where have you been?' She replied 'In the barn looking for some iron.' She said she was afraid her father had had trouble with the tenants, and she had overheard loud conversation several times recently. ... I asked for a sheet to cover up Mr. Borden. Bridget brought me one. Then Miss Lizzie asked me to telegraph to her sister Emma, and I went to the telegraph office."

By this time, the big question was how to get word to Abby that her husband was dead, but of course, that would not end up being necessary. Sullivan remembered discovering Abby's body: "And I says, 'Oh, Lizzie, if I knew where Mrs. Whitehead was I would go and see if Mrs. Borden was there and tell her that Mr. Borden was very sick.' She says, 'Maggie, I am almost positive I heard her coming in. Won't you go upstairs to see?' I said, 'I am not going upstairs alone.' I had been upstairs already after sheets for Dr. Bowen. ... Mrs. Churchill said she would go upstairs with me. As I went upstairs, I saw the body under the bed. I ran right into the room and stood at the foot of the bed. The door of the room was open. I did not stop or make any examination. Mrs. Churchill did not go in the room. We came right down. Miss Lizzie was in the dining room, lying on the lounge."

Pictures of Abby's body

Chapter 4: The Investigation

"There was no blood visible on Lizzie at the time her father was discovered. There was never any blood found on Lizzie's clothes... Although at least four hatchets and axes were discovered in the cellar, no blood was found on any of them. There was a broken hatchet presented at trial as a possible murder weapon, but it was little more than a theory which was discounted by the defense. Actually, there were only the conflicting statements, her strange reactions, and her behavior that made Lizzie Borden highly suspect. There was never any physical evidence that tied anyone in the house to the murders. Bridget, Lizzie and a hypothetical intruder all had an opportunity to have done the crime. The police never looked for another killer. They searched Lizzie's dresses for blood spatter evidence, but apparently did not search Bridget's clothes." - Trey Wyatt, *The Life, Legend, and Mystery of Lizzie Borden.*

Within minutes, the Borden home was swarming with police, and the officers immediately contacted Dr. William Dolan. Dolan had "been medical examiner for Bristol County for two years; for one year, when these murders took place," and he noted, "Arrived at the Borden house about 11:45 A.M. ... Saw Charles Sawyer at the door; Dr. Bowen, Bridget, Mr. Morse, Mrs. Churchill, Miss Russell, and several officers."

Medical Examiner William A. Dolan

Dolan

It fell to Dr. Dolan to do the preliminary autopsies while the bodies remained in place. He noted, "The body of Mr. Borden was lying on the sofa. ... I found that Mr. Borden's hand was warm; the blood was oozing from his wounds and was bright red in color. The head was resting on a sofa cushion that had a little white tidy on it. The cushion, I think, rested on his coat, which had been doubled up and put under there. And the coat, in turn, rested on an afghan or sofa cover. I made no particular examination of the wounds then; only stayed two or three minutes; went upstairs to see Mrs. Borden. She was lying between the dressing case and the bed. I touched the body, noted the wounds on the back of her head; noted that her blood was coagulated and of a dark color. She was lying with her back exposed; her hands were nearer the wall than her head; they were not clasped. The upper part of her dress, the waist, was bloody. I found an old silk handkerchief there and took it with me. It was nearer the wall than the head. It was not cut, but it was bloodstained. I was there, examining the body, for only two or three minutes. When I saw Mr. Borden I had a clinical thermometer with me, but I did not use it. At Mr. Borden's head, the blood was dripping on the carpet underneath. There were two blood spots on the carpet, about eight or ten inches in diameter."

It did not take Dr. Dolan long to determine that Abby had died first. He later explained, "Turning back to Mrs. Borden's body, I felt of that with my hand; touched her head and hand; it was much colder than that of Mr. Borden. Did not use thermometer. Her blood on the head was matted and practically dry. There was no oozing from it, as in Mr. Borden's...I returned downstairs and made a more careful observation of Mr. Borden's wounds. At that time I counted from eight to ten; I made a more accurate examination later. He was clad in a cardigan, a woolen jacket, black vest, black trousers and a pair of Congress shoes. He had a watch and pocketbook; the money in the pocketbook amounted to $81.65.... He wore a ring, I think a gold ring on his left hand. Went upstairs again, and with Dr. Bowen's assistance lifted Mrs. Borden's body sufficiently to make a preliminary count of her wounds; then collected from Bridget a sample of the morning's milk and of yesterday's milk; sealed them and later sent them to Professor Wood. Went to the cellar; saw two axes and two hatchets; took the heavy claw-hammered one and put it with the cans of milk. Returned to the house that afternoon and had the rooms and the two bodies photographed."

Deputy Marshal John Fleet questioned Lizzie that day and subsequently testified that Lizzie had claimed to be in the barn looking for sinkers to take with her on a planned fishing trip. Lizzie herself made the same claim at her inquest. She also recounted to him the same story she had told Russell the previous evening about a strange man who came to the house. When asked about her mother's body, Lizzie gave what was perhaps the first hint of the tension in the house by insisting, "She is not my mother, sir, she is my step-mother; my mother died when I was a child."

As the initial investigative work was being done, Morse returned to the house: "I walked around behind the house and picked some pears. Then I went in the back door. Bridget then told me that Mr. and Mrs. Borden bad been murdered. I opened the sitting-room door and found a number of people including the doctors. I entered, but only glanced once at the body. ... Then I went upstairs and took a similar hasty view of the dead woman. Everything is confusion, however, and I recall very little of what took place."

After completing their preliminary investigations, the police left, leaving neighbor Alice Russell at the house with Lizzie, Sullivan and Morse. Russell later testified, "I stayed at the house all that night, having gone home once that day and returned. I did not suggest to Miss Lizzie that she change her dress; did not hear anyone suggest it. Thursday night [August 4], I went down into the cellar with Lizzie; I carried a lamp, she carried a slop pail. Went to the water closet. The clothing taken from the bodies was in the washroom. Miss Lizzie went into the washroom; I did not. She went to the sink there and rinsed out the pail. Then we went upstairs again. I stayed at the house from the day of the murders till Monday morning. I was there Thursday, Friday, Saturday and Sunday nights. On Thursday and Friday nights, I occupied Mr. and Mrs. Borden's room; Saturday and Sunday nights, Miss Emma Borden's room."

Emma rushed home as soon as she heard what had happened, and together she and Lizzie planned the quiet funeral that was held in the home on Saturday. However, their trip from the house to the burial was far from quiet, as the town turned out to watch the procession. All eyes were on Lizzie that day, and *The Boston Herald* reported, "[A]s she was stepping into the carriage to follow her parents remains to the cemetery…it seemed as if she was well-deserving of the encomiums of her friends and of the kind words which follow. She makes an exceedingly favorable impression and her dignity and her reserve are at once impressed. It was a trying ordeal to pass before the eyes of a crowd of 1500 morbidly curious spectators. She wore a tight fitting black lace dress with a plain skirt and waist of equally modest cut and finish, while a dark hat, trimmed with similar material, rested upon her head. Of medium height, she is possessed of a symmetrical figure with a retiring manner and a carriage which would dignifiedly repel the attention. A wealth of black hair is revealed under the hat which, arranged on top of her head, is trained about her forehead in short curls, parted in the centre and thrown over to the sides. Her dark, lustrous eyes, ordinarily flashing, were dimmed, and her pale face was evidence of the physical suffering she was undergoing and had experienced. To sum up, Miss Lizzie Borden, without a word from herself in her own defence, is a strong argument in her own favor."

Meanwhile, back at the Borden house, the police were taking advantage of the family's absence to search the place. Russell remembered, "Officers did come in the house, during the absence of the funeral party, but they didn't come as soon as the party left. They made a search, but they didn't search everywhere. They went into Miss Lizzie's room. ... I think one of the officers took the keys that lay on the bureau after Miss Lizzie had left and unlocked one or two drawers in her bureau, and didn't search any farther there. I think they opened what she called her toilet room, pulled the portiere one side, just looked there a little. I don't know how much they searched. I don't think very much; and they went into Miss Emma's room and looked around, and opened the cupboard door in her room, and I remember one of the officers pressing against a bundle after he shut it, some pillow or blanket, something of that kind, and the bed was taken to pieces."

The next morning, Lizzie did something that would permanently incriminate her in the eyes of many. Russell explained, "On Sunday morning, I got the breakfast. After breakfast, I left the lower part of the house for a while, returning before noon. I went into the kitchen, and I saw Miss Lizzie at the other end of the stove; I saw Miss Emma at the sink. Miss Lizzie was at the stove, and she had a skirt in her hand, and her sister turned and said, 'What are you going to do?' and Lizzie said, 'I am going to burn this old thing up; it is covered with paint.' ... [Later,] Miss Lizzie stood up towards the cupboard door; the cupboard door was open, and she appeared to be either ripping something down or tearing part of this garment. ... I said to her, 'I wouldn't let anybody see me do that, Lizzie.' She didn't make any answer. ... She stepped just one step farther back up towards the cupboard door. I didn't know that it was the waist, but I saw a portion of this dress up on the cupboard shelf."

Within 24 hours it became clear that Lizzie had made a serious mistake in burning that dress. Her sister Emma later told the court, "Miss Russell came to us in the dining room [Monday] and said Mr. Hanscom (one of the investigators) asked her if all the dresses were there that were there the day of the tragedy, and she told him 'Yes,' 'and of course,' she said, 'it is a falsehood.' No, I am ahead of my story. She came and said she told Mr. Hanscom a falsehood, and I asked her what there was to tell a falsehood about, and then she said that Mr. Hanscom had asked her if all the dresses were there that were there the day of the tragedy and she told him 'Yes.' There was other conversation, but I don't know what it was. That frightened me so thoroughly, I cannot recall it. I know the carriage was waiting for her to go on some errand, and when she came back we had some conversation and it was decided to have her go and tell Mr. Hanscom that she had told a falsehood, and to tell him that we told her to do so. She went into the parlor and told him, and in a few minutes she returned from the parlor and said she had told him."

On Tuesday, August 9, less than a week after the murders, *The Fall River Herald* reported, "The central police station was the center of all interest in the Borden case Monday afternoon and night. Rumors of arrests were thick in the air, and there was a hustling and bustling that indicated that something was going to be done. Officers hurried to and fro with an anxious look on their faces. Everybody was on the qui vive, and it was expected that a sensation might occur at any moment, but the moments dragged along into hours and nothing happened. ... It was known that City Marshal Hilliard and his allies had reached the point where they needed legal advice and that the marshal had sent for Hosea M. Knowlton, the district attorney. Shortly after 5 o'clock the district attorney came. He held a brief consultation with the marshal, a long talk with Medical Examiner Dolan, and again it looked as if a move was about to be made. ... Excitement bubbled up and boiled over. Then it died down [a] little. District Attorney Knowlton went out to the Mellen house to supper. At 8 o'clock Marshal Hilliard and State Officer Seaver left the central station and walked to the hotel. They met the medical examiner, and with the district attorney reviewed the case from beginning to end."

Knowlton

Hilliard

The clothing issue continued to be of concern. According to *The Herald*, on Tuesday the 9th, "Medical Examiner Dolan went to the Borden house in the afternoon and had the clothing worn by the victims of the murder dug up and spread on the grass for examination. There were certain parts that he wanted for further investigation, and he carried them away with him and had the remnants buried behind the barn. Mr. Morse walked down town in the afternoon and paused on his way to and from the post office to converse with friends whom he met. Nobody interfered with him, but Officer Devine never lost sight of him for an Instant. There was nothing going on about the Borden premises to attract attention except the squad of policemen who are still kept on guard about the place."

Chapter 5: Inquest, Arrest, Indictment

"It was interesting that Lizzie would not say, at the inquest, that all was cordial even though it would have been to her advantage and there weren't a lot of people to dispute it. ... Her defiance and resolve was interesting. She truly did not seem to remember some of the details of the day and many of the things she remembered did not happen (like her father putting on his slippers) and had no bearing whatsoever on the case. The inquest testimony is what led to Lizzie Borden's arrest. Actually there was never any murder weapon found, not a speck of blood found on Lizzie or in her room, and no real evidence of a motive. The behavior and statements of Lizzie Borden both directly after and in the following days (including the inquest) were the main reason that Lizzie was arrested. ... It cannot be overstated how much Lizzie's erratic and bizarre behavior and conflicting statements in the days following the crime, all the way through the inquest, were largely responsible for her arrest and prosecution. With no physical evidence and general speculation, as to motive the case moved forward." - Trey Wyatt, *The Life, Legend, and Mystery of Lizzie Borden*

On the evening of the 9th, the inquest began. *The Herald* reported, "About 5:30 o'clock the marshal's private wire let the telephone bell ringing, and a voice announced that the district attorney was at the Mellen house and ready to begin business. Taking the big box under his arm, Marshal Hilliard started out of the office with Detective Seaver close to his heels. They walked rapidly up to the hotel and met the district attorney in parlor on the second floor. ... The most important papers were selected from the bundle, and the three men discussed the case in an in formal way. An hour was finally set at 10 o'clock to meet in the same place to review the entire situation in a systematic way and to determine how to proceed. At that hour the men got together again, Mayor Coughlin and Medical Examiner Dolan being with them. All hands took off their coats and settled to the task in hand without any preliminary delay. The marshal began at the beginning and continued to the end."

During the inquest, the first evidence that impeached Lizzie's statements came to light. According to *The Herald*, "On the day of the murder Miss Lizzie had explained that she went to the loft of the barn for the lead, and an officer who was examining the premises also went to the loft. It was covered with dust and there were no tracks to prove that any person had been there for weeks. He took particular notice of the fact, and reported back that he had walked about on the dust-covered floor on purpose to discover whether or not his own feet left any tracks. He said that they did and thought it singular that anybody could have visited the floor a short time before him and make no impressions on the dust. The lower floor of the stable told no such tale, as it was evident that it had been used more frequently and the dust had not accumulated there." Sympathetic to a woman of good reputation in the town, *The Herald* noted, "The conclusion reached was that in the excitement incident to the awful discovery, Miss Borden had forgotten just where she went for the lead."

Then there was the question of why Lizzie did not call out for Abby when she found her father dead. Lizzie explained this away by maintaining that she believed Abby had already been called out of the house, but it again came to light that the letter asking for her help was never found.

With these facts in mind, the inquest continued. *The Herald* wrote, "The marshal, medical examiner and the mayor carefully rehearsed, step by step, the summoning of Dr. Bowen, who was not at home when the murder was committed, and his ghastly discovery on the second floor. No theory other than that Mrs. Borden was murdered first was entertained, and. Mayor Coughlin was positive that the murderer had closed the door after the deed had been accomplished. Lizzie Borden's demeanor during the many interviews which the police have had with her was described at length, and the story of John W. Morse's whereabouts was retold. As the night wore on it began to grow very certain that nothing would be done. There was no excuse for doing it at that hour. The persons to whom the only suspicions of any account were pointed were already under arrest for all intents and purposes. If there had been no reason why they should have been arrested in the day time it was certain that no new discoveries had been made that would compel the police to act before daylight came around again, and the wiser night-hawks on the lookout for news flew home to bed."

The next morning, the inquest proceeded with witnesses being called. According to *The Herald*, "Bridget Sullivan, the domestic, was the first to arrive at the station. ... From the time Miss Sullivan went up stairs, 9:45 o'clock, until 11:20 nothing indicated that an inquest was being held. An officer was placed at the head of the stairs and no one was allowed to approach within hearing distance of the room. At the time mentioned Judge Blaisdell came from the court and hurried toward his law office."

Next came Lizzie herself. The article continued, "At 1:45 o'clock Marshal Hilliard and Officer Harrington left the central station in one of Stone's hacks. The uniform of the marshal as he drove up Second Street attracted the attention of pedestrians, and in less time than it takes to write fully 500 people had assembled on the opposite side of the street facing the Borden mansion. Mrs. George Brigham left the house and was seen to enter Dr. Bowen's office. The supposition immediately became general that Lizzie, whom the officers wished to convey as a witness in the inquest, had broken down under the strain. Such was not the case however, as when she came to take her place in the carriage her step was light and, other than a care-worn expression, nothing indicated the terrible mental strain that she was undergoing."

At this time, the reporter remained somewhat sympathetic: "In the past few days Lizzie has terribly aged. The full round cheeks that friends of her former days remember have entirely disappeared, although the bright eyes and haughty expression are still retained. There was not a falter in the step as she came down the stairs, and from her every movement the woman would be the last person to suspect of the crime. In fact, her step was such as would indicate that she was going to a picnic instead of attending an inquest. All along the road crowds of people had gathered, and when the hack turned back toward the station there was a mad rush for the alley. The four passengers slighted from the hack and passed into the station, going at once to the court room above. After they had passed up the stairs, Officer Barker took his place on the landing and forbade anybody passing the staircase beyond the clerk's office. In the court room were Judge Blaisdell, Marshal Hilliard, Dr. Dolan, Detective Seaver and the district attorney. Andrew Jennings went into the marshal's office, but was not present at the inquest. Miss Borden was questioned closely as to her doings and those of the rest of the family."

The inquest proved to be Lizzie's undoing, as she was unable to give clear answers to many of the questions put to her. In fact, she often tripped over her own answers and made conflicting statements. Thus, after questioning other witnesses, the board instructed Marshal Hilliard to arrest her. The August 11 edition of *The New York Times* reported, "Lizzie Borden is under arrest charged with murdering her father and step-mother last Thursday morning at their home on Second Street. She was brought into the Second District Court room about 3 o'clock this afternoon, presumably to give further evidence at the inquest. Miss Borden was accompanied by her sister and Mrs. Brigham. ... When Miss Lizzie returned from the third inquiry she was a physical and mental wreck and was conducted to the matron's room. The inquest was adjourned about 4 o'clock. District Attorney Knowlton and other officials went to the Marshal's private office, where they remained closeted for two hours. Shortly after 6 o'clock City Marshal Hilliard and District Attorney Knowlton drove to the home of Andrew Jennings, who had been the family's attorney for some years. They returned at about 7 o'clock, and went into the matron's room, where Lizzie was lying on the sofa. The reading of the warrant was waived. The lady took the announcement of her arrest with surprising calmness. Two women who were with her were much more visibly affected. The excitement on the street was very great when the news of the arrest became known, although some hours previous it was generally understood that Miss Borden was soon to be made a prisoner. Miss Borden was scarched by Mrs. Russell shortly after she was formally placed in custody."

On August 12, Lizzie appeared before Judge Josiah Blaisdell and pleaded not guilty to the charges against her. She was then jailed in Taunton, a small town about eight miles from Fall River, presumably because of the attention the case was drawing.

10 days later, Lizzie appeared in court again for a preliminary hearing. After considering the charges against her, Judge Blaisdell determined she was "probably guilty" and passed her case on to the Grand Jury.

Initially, the Grand Jury concluded that there was insufficient evidence to warrant an indictment. Even Hilliard had earlier told *The New York Times* "that three clues were already being run down and none of them would in any way implicate a member of the household. … It has been proved that the milk drank by the Borden family was not poisoned when it was taken from the Borden farm and brought to the city. Members of the family in charge of the farm drank it, and they were affected in no noticeable way."

However, when Sullivan testified that Lizzie had been wearing a blue dress on the morning of the murders, and Russell testified about the blue dress Lizzie burned, the jurors changed their minds. On December 2, 1892, they indicted her.

INDICTMENT.

COMMONWEALTH
vs.
LIZZIE ANDREW BORDEN.

MURDER.

Commonwealth of Massachusetts.

BRISTOL SS. *At the Superior Court begun and holden at Taunton within and for said County of Bristol, on the first Monday of November, in the year of our Lord one thousand eight hundred and ninety-two.*

The Jurors for the said Commonwealth, on their oath present,—That Lizzie Andrew Borden of Fall River in the County of Bristol, at Fall River in the County of Bristol, on the fourth day of August in the year eighteen hundred and ninety-two, in and upon one Andrew Jackson Borden, feloniously, wilfully and of her malice aforethought, an assault did make, and with a certain weapon, to wit, a sharp cutting instrument, the name and a more particular description of which is to the Jurors unknown, him, the said Andrew Jackson Borden feloniously, wilfully and of her malice aforethought, did strike, cut, beat and bruise, in and upon the head of him, the said Andrew Jackson Borden, giving to him, the said Andrew Jackson Borden, by the said striking, cutting, beating and bruising, in and upon the head of him, the said Andrew Jackson Borden, divers, to wit, ten mortal wounds, of which said mortal wounds the said Andrew Jackson Borden then and there instantly died.

And so the Jurors aforesaid, upon their oath aforesaid, do say, that the said Lizzie Andrew Borden, the said Andrew Jackson Borden, in manner and form aforesaid, then and there feloniously, wilfully and of her malice aforethought did kill and murder; against the peace of said Commonwealth and contrary to the form of the statute in such case made and provided.

A true bill.

HENRY A. BODMAN,

HOSEA M. KNOWLTON,   Foreman of the Grand Jury.

District Attorney.

Bristol ss. On this second day of December, in the year eighteen hundred and ninety-two, this indictment was returned and presented to said Superior Court by the Grand Jury, ordered to be filed, and filed; and it was further ordered by the Court that notice be given to said Lizzie Andrew Borden that said indictment will be entered forthwith upon the docket of the Superior Court in said County.

Attest:—

SIMEON BORDEN, Jr.,

Asst. Clerk.

A true copy.
Attest: *Simeon Borden* Clerk.

A copy of the indictment

Chapter 6: The Trial

"During her trial and incarceration, the press was overall favorable and respectful towards Lizzie Borden. The sentiment was that Lizzie was being railroaded by the police and an ambitious prosecutor. There was a lot of coverage that reflected the belief that Lizzie wasn't 'strong' enough to have committed the crime and that women didn't kill with a hatchet. The coverage of the trial was so detailed, in many papers that it devoted up to six pages of verbatim testimony. Public opinion swayed back and forth daily depending on the testimony and evidence presented. The murders were covered internationally. The trial drew reporters from all over the world. ... The local newspapers, especially the Fall River Herald stayed firmly in her corner. She was embraced as one of Fall River's finest until she was acquitted. Lizzie decided to stay in Fall River and make it her home. The friends who had stood by her during her trial turned their backs on her after she moved up on 'The Hill.'" - Trey Wyatt, *The Life, Legend, and Mystery of Lizzie Borden.*

By the time Lizzie's trial began on June 5, 1893, the entire nation was mesmerized by the case. Inside the New Bedford Courthouse was a panel of three judges: Chief Justice Albert Mason, Judge Caleb Blodgett, and Judge Justin Dewey. Knowlton and Thomas Moody were there to prosecute the case, while well-known attorneys Andrew Jennings and George Robinson (who was previously the Governor of Massachusetts) had been hired by Emma to defend her sister.

Moody

Jennings

Robinson

A picture of the jury

The drama of the case was lost on no one, and, after the jury was seated, Moody came out swinging on June 6: "There was or came to be between prisoner and stepmother an unkindly feeling. From the nature of the case it will be impossible for us to get anything more than suggestive glimpses of this feeling from outsiders. The daughters thought that something should be done for them by way of dividing the property after they had learned that the stepmother had been amply provided for. Then came a division and ill-feeling, and the title of 'mother' was dropped. ... 'When, an officer was seeking information from the prisoner, right in sight of the woman who had sunken under the assassin's blows, and asked, 'When did you last see your mother?' the reply came from Lizzie: ' 'She isn't my mother; my mother died when I was an infant.'"

After speaking for two hours, Moody concluded, "The time for hasty and inexact reasoning is past. We are to be guided from this time forth by the law and the evidence only. I adjure you gentlemen to keep your minds in the same open attitude which you have maintained to-day to the end. When that end comes, after you have heard the evidence on both sides, the arguments of the counsel and the instruction of the court, God forbid that you should step one step against the law or beyond the evidence. But if your minds, considering all these circumstances, are irresistibly brought to the conclusion of the guilt of the prisoner, we ask you in your verdict to declare her guilty. By so doing, shall you make true deliverance of the great issue which has been submitted to you." At this point, Lizzie fainted and had to be revived with smelling salts.

Of all the witnesses present during the trial, none was as important as Bridget Sullivan, the only other person known to be in the house that day. She told the jury of the illnesses the family had experienced, her efforts washing the windows, and how Lizzie had so suddenly summoned her. She also discussed finding Abby's body and going for help. She was one of the few who appeared who spoke well of Lizzie's and Abby's relationship, assuring the jury she had witnessed nothing uncordial between them.

After Sullivan left the stand, Morse came forward and offered his own testimony about what happened during the morning of the murders before he left the house.

Once prosecutors had called the people who actually lived in the house, the prosecution next called to the stand those who had investigated the murders. Dr. Bowen repeated his conversations with Lizzie about the sinkers and the tenants that she claimed were so upset with her father. He also admitted that he had prescribed morphine for her following the murders and speculated that the drug might have contributed to her confused state during the time the police were questioning her. Adelaide Churchill admitted that, while Lizzie was wearing a blue dress similar to the one she was said to have burned, she never saw a spot of blood on either the dress or her hands, adding that even Lizzie's hair was tidy. The other important witness in the case was Alice Russell. After sharing information about Lizzie's strange visit to her home the night before the murders, she talked about how she witnessed Lizzie burning the dress. At the same time, she also noted, "I saw no blood on that dress. Not a drop. The edge of the dress was soiled. I did not actually see her put it in the stove."

Considering everything, the state's case was surprisingly weak, a fact that the defense was only too happy to point out. The judges disallowed the testimony about Lizzie supposedly trying to buy cyanide, ruling, "It is the opinion of the court that the preliminary proceedings have not been sufficient..." They also disallowed Lizzie's testimony made during her inquest since she had no lawyer present.

After thoroughly dismantling the testimonies of witnesses that the prosecution had called, the defense rose to present its own case on June 15. Among the few witnesses they called was Dr. Benjamin Handy, a family friend of the Borden's. He testified, "I went by the Borden house, on the morning of the murders, at nine o'clock, and again at a little after 10.30. Saw a medium-sized young man of very pale complexion, with his eyes fixed on the side-walk. He was passing slowly towards the south. He was paler than common, and acting strangely. I turned in my carriage to look at him. Never have seen him before. Had light suit of clothes, collar and necktie. Have searched for him since; been to the police station to look at various persons; but have never seen the young man since. ... He was walking very slowly, scarcely moving. He was agitated, or weak, staggering; or confused, or something of the kind. Did not appear intoxicated. Seemed mentally agitated: showed this by intense expression of his face. I think I had seen him on some previous day. He did not stagger. ... His body oscillated."

Fall River citizens Charles Gifford and Uriah Kirby offered similar testimony, also claiming to have seen a strange man near the Borden house on the morning of the murders.

The defense also called in two different workmen who testified that they had been in the barn's loft on during the days leading up to the murders. This indicated that the police would have been wrong in asserting there were no footprints in the dust up there.

According to Joe Howard, writing for the *Boston Globe*, "Next to the interest felt in Lizzie Borden, with a possible exception in favor of well-meaning Bridget Sullivan, the popular desire has been greatest to see Miss Emma Borden, daughter of the murdered man and sister of the accused." When she was called to testify on June 16, the last day of the trial, all eyes were on her as she spoke out in defense of her sister. According to the article, "She first gave an itemized list of Lizzie's property, amounting to deposits in sundry savings banks of about $2500, two shares in the Fall River national bank and nine shares in the Merchants manufacturing company. She said that the gold ring on Borden's finger was given to him by Lizzie 10 or 15 years ago, she having worn it a long time, and that he prized it highly and always kept it on his little finger, where it was when he was buried. She produced an inventory of 18 or 19 dresses hanging in their clothes press, and swore in response to marshal Fleet's assertion that the search didn't amount to much, that Dr. Dolan told her they had searched from attic to cellar, Bridget taking the paper from the walls and the carpets from the floors. ... Mr. Knowlton's ingenious cross-examination endeavored to prove a condition of ill feeling in the Borden household, but succeeded only as far as the witness herself was concerned."

In his summation, Jennings argued that "there is not one particle of direct evidence in this case from beginning to end against Lizzie A. Borden. There is not a spot of blood, there is not a weapon that they have connected with her in any way, shape or fashion." Robinson then added that only someone strong and insane could have committed the crime, certainly not the prim spinster the jurors saw before them.

After Knowlton summed up the prosecution's case, Justice Dewey took over. He charged the jury in such a way that, as Howard put it, if he had "been the senior counsel for the defense, making the closing plea in behalf of the defendant, he could not have more absolutely pointed out the folly of depending upon circumstantial evidence alone." After just 90 minutes of deliberation, the jury returned a verdict of "Not Guilty." Crying out and then collapsing back into her chair, Lizzie was soon in her sister's comforting arms, from which she was heard to say, "Now take me home. I want to go to the old place and go at once tonight."

The trial of the year was over, but the case was far from decided. *The New York Times* praised the verdict: "It will be a certain relief to every right-minded man or woman who has followed the case to learn that the jury at New Bedford has not only acquitted Miss Lizzie Borden of the atrocious crime with which she was charged, but has done so with a promptness that was very significant." In fact, it is likely that the prejudices of the day worked in Lizzie's favor, as no one could believe a woman capable of such an offence.

Lizzie and Emma lived for a time together in Fall River in a large mansion they purchased with their inheritance. However, Emma moved out in 1905, leaving Lizzie to entertain the largely bohemian friends she came to surround herself with. Both women died in 1927, Lizzie first at the age of 67, and Emma less than two weeks later.

A picture of Lizzie later in life

Of course, in the nearly 90 years since Lizzie died, her notoriety has only grown as the compelling story has been endlessly pored over in print and on screen. While the Borden house becoming a bed and breakfast/museum, historians and other writers have posited various theories to either explain how Lizzie committed the murders and got away with them or how someone else managed to kill Andrew and Abby. Others have dramatized the story, such as Alfred Hitchcock, who presented an episode on *Alfred Hitchcock Presents* that had Lizzie covering for her sister Emma.

Regardless, with the case remaining unsolved, it's safe to say that the interest of the last 120 years will not abate any time soon.

Online Resources

Other books about 19th century American history by Charles River Editors

Other books about Lizzie Borden on Amazon

Bibliography

Brown, Arnold R. *Lizzie Borden: The Legend, the Truth, the Final Chapter.* Nashville, TN: Rutledge Hill Press, 1991,

de Mille, Agnes. *Lizzie Borden: A Dance of Death.* Boston: Little, Brown and Co., 1968.

Kent, David *Forty Whacks: New Evidence in the Life and Legend of Lizzie Borden.* Yankee Books, 1992,

The Lizzie Borden Sourcebook. Boston: Branden Publishing Company, 1992,

Masterton, William L. *Lizzie Didn't Do It!* Boston: Branden Publishing Company, 2000,

Pearson, Edmund Lester. *Trial of Lizzie Borden, edited, with a history of the case*, Doubleday-Doran, 1937.

Rebello, Leonard. *Lizzie Borden: Past & Present* Al-Zach Press, 1999.

Rehak, David. *Did Lizzie Borden Axe For It?* Angel Dust Publishing, 2008.

Spiering, Frank. *Lizzie: The Story of Lizzie Borden.* Dorset Press, 1991.

Sullivan, Robert. *Goodbye Lizzie Borden.* Brattleboro, VT: Stephen Greene Press, 1974.

Wyatt, Trey. *Lizzie Borden - The Life, Legend, And Mystery of Lizzie Borden,* Amazon Digital Services, Inc. 2014.

Made in the USA
Columbia, SC
24 October 2017